Taming The Storm.

Taming the Storm

Hasan Clay

Understanding and overcoming high-conflict personalities, for a peaceful life

The content in this book is intended for informational and educational purposes only and does not constitute professional medical advice, diagnosis, or treatment. The techniques, strategies, and suggestions presented in this book are based on the author's research and experience and are intended to support general wellbeing. This book is not a substitute for professional mental health care, therapy, or counselling.

If you are experiencing emotional or mental health challenges, please consult a licensed healthcare provider, therapist, or counsellor for guidance and support. Always seek the advice of your physician or other qualified mental health provider with any questions you may have regarding a medical or psychological condition.

ISBN: 978-1-7326735-1-9

DEDICATION:

First and foremost, I want to thank ***Bill Eddy*** for pioneering the concept of high-conflict personalities. Though I've never had the pleasure of meeting him, his work has profoundly influenced this journey.

I am equally grateful to two remarkable women, ***Sumayyah and Naaila,*** who inspired me to delve into this research, each for unique reasons.

To those who have stood by me—***Shadeed Muhammed, Zayd Ansari, and Kaleema Overton Amin***—your unwavering support has been invaluable.

And to the world's greatest VA, ***Odile Theunissen*** your dedication and tireless work ethic have been the backbone of this book's creation.

Finally, to everyone I hold dear, and to those who hold me in their hearts, know that I am eternally grateful to you all. I may be absentminded at times, but never absent in heart.

— Hasan.

Pre-Assessment:

Purpose of the Pre-Assessment.

Before you begin reading, it's essential to understand where you currently stand in your ability to manage conflict and emotional triggers. This pre-assessment serves as a tool to help you reflect on your experiences and skills related to conflict management, giving you a baseline to measure your growth as you progress through the book.

By taking a few minutes to complete this pre-assessment, you will:

Enhance Self-Awareness:

Understand your current conflict management style and identify areas where you excel and those that may need improvement.

Personalize Your Experience:

Tailor the book's exercises and strategies to fit your specific needs, ensuring a more impactful reading experience.

Track Your Progress:

Compare your pre-assessment results with the post-assessment at the end of the book to measure your growth and celebrate improvements.

Pre- Assessment Instructions:

Rate each of the following scenarios based on your current experiences using the scale below:

= **Very Unlikely**: This scenario almost never occurs (e.g., you rarely find yourself in conflicts).

= **Unlikely**: This happens occasionally, but it's not a frequent issue (e.g., you sometimes feel uncomfortable expressing emotions).

= **Sometimes**: This scenario occurs with moderate frequency (e.g., you occasionally misinterpret others' intentions).

= **Likely**: This happens often, but not always (e.g., you frequently feel emotional triggers during conflicts).

= **Very Likely**: This scenario happens consistently (e.g., you often find conflict difficult to manage).

Pre-Assessment Questions:

How often do you find yourself in arguments or conflicts with others?

(Rarely, or Frequently)

When you argue, do you find it difficult to let go until you feel you've "won" the argument?

(Never, or Always)

How comfortable are you with expressing your emotions during disagreements

(Very uncomfortable, or Very comfortable)

When others disagree with you, do you often feel personally attacked?

(Never, or Always)

Do you tend to avoid conflict altogether, even if it means sacrificing your own needs or opinions?

(1 = Never, or Always)

How well do you feel you understand the emotional triggers that cause conflict for you?

(Not at all, or Completely)

On a scale of 1 to 5, how often do you believe you misinterpret others' intentions during a disagreement?

(Never , or Frequently)

Do you find it difficult to maintain relationships with people who have high-conflict personalities?

(Not at all, or Very difficult)

How comfortable are you with setting boundaries in your personal relationships?

(Very uncomfortable, or Very comfortable).

How confident are you that conflict can be managed and turned into an opportunity for growth?

(Not confident at all, or Very confident)

Scoring Guide.

After answering each question, add up your scores to find your total. Refer to the guide below to interpret your results:

Scores of 35-50:
You have a solid understanding of high-conflict behaviour and likely manage conflict well in certain areas of your life. This book will help you deepen your skills, especially in recognizing emotional triggers and refining how you set boundaries with high conflict individuals.

Scores of 20-34:
You encounter moderate levels of conflict and may struggle to identify the deeper emotional roots behind your reactions. This book offers tools to enhance your emotional intelligence, communication skills, and confidence in managing difficult situations effectively.

Scores of 10-19:
You may feel overwhelmed by conflict and uncertain about how to navigate it. This book will provide foundational strategies to help you understand your own high-conflict tendencies and those of others, empowering you to regain control and build healthier interactions.

WORKBOOK and PERSONAL JOURNAL:

This workbook and personal reflection journal are designed to accompany the book *Taming the Storm: Understanding and Overcoming High-Conflict Personalities for a Peaceful Life*, offering practical exercises, tools, and space for personal growth. Each chapter is followed by a dedicated section that includes reflection questions, action steps, and activities to help you apply the concepts from the book to your daily life, enhancing your emotional intelligence, communication skills, and conflict management. After each chapter, you'll find journal prompts to guide you through personal reflections, allowing you to explore your experiences, emotions, and progress. Additionally, at the end of the book, you'll find a comprehensive journal section where you can continue documenting your thoughts, insights, and growth as you move forward on your journey to peace and healthier relationships.

Journal instructions:

Daily Reflections:
After reading each chapter, use the journal to reflect on your key takeaways and how they apply to your life.

Emotional Tracking:
Identify and track emotional triggers, patterns, and responses.

Conflict Logging:
Record specific conflicts to analyse your reactions and learn from each interaction.

Goal Setting:
Use the space to set personal goals for improvement and track your journey beyond the book.

Foreword:

Welcome to the fascinating world of social psychology, where everyday interactions become windows into the human soul, and ordinary moments reveal extraordinary truths about who we are.

This book will take you on a journey through the hidden forces that shape our thoughts, feelings, and behaviours in social settings.

Imagine walking into a room, and, without a word, feeling the mood shift based on a single person's presence. Or consider how deeply your behaviour can be swayed by the simple pressure of a group. Social psychology uncovers the science behind these subtle powers— why we conform, how stereotypes form, what influences attraction, and the surprising ways we can be persuaded to act against our own interests.

In this phenomenal work of intellectual art, Hasan Clay soothes your curiosities about high conflict personalities. With an easily digestible literary style, he explains how changes in our thoughts not only shape entire conversations but entire interactions. This book will unlock the mysteries behind human behaviour and relationships.

By the time you finish, you'll see yourself, your friends, and even strangers on the street in a new light—aware of the invisible scripts and forces at play in every social interaction. This is more than a book; it's a toolkit for understanding humanity.

Turn the page, and step into your own mind and the minds of others.

Aqil Ingram.

Introduction:

Conflict can feel like a storm—sudden, fierce, and seemingly beyond control. It can tear through relationships, leaving behind hurt, broken communication, and a sense of powerlessness. For some, this storm rages constantly, fuelled by deep emotional triggers or fears. For others, it's brought into their lives by people they care about—partners, family members, or colleagues—who turn even the smallest disagreement into a battle. But here's the truth: the storm doesn't have to define you. It can be tamed.

In ***Taming the Storm: Understanding and Overcoming High-Conflict Personalities for a Peaceful Life***, you'll not only find explanations for why conflict arises but also tools to transform it. This book isn't about avoiding conflict or pretending it doesn't exist; it's about understanding the roots of high-conflict behaviour, addressing underlying fears, and learning how to navigate these challenges with intention and compassion.

You'll encounter real stories of people who faced the storm of high conflict behaviour and learned how to calm the storms. You'll discover why some individuals are prone to conflict and gain strategies to manage these patterns, whether they surface in your own behaviour or those around you. In this book you will not only find scenarios but a workbook and a journal after each chapter for you to reflect on and jot down your thoughts. This book is about empowerment, offering you a path to reclaim peace in your relationships and within yourself.

A Personal Note

I understand what it's like to navigate emotional storms. My own journey, filled with challenges and triumphs, taught me how to find peace amid chaos. I've combined my personal experiences and professional expertise to give you practical tools that have helped countless others reclaim their lives.

Imagine a life where conversations don't escalate into battles, where disagreements lead to understanding instead of disconnection. The storm doesn't have to control you. You can navigate it, calm it, and rise above it.

Are you ready to tame the storm? Let's begin.

CHAPTER ONE. Born from Chaos.

The Roots of High-Conflict Behaviour.

High-conflict behaviour often stems from a turbulent past, where instability, fear, or hurt took root, shaping how individuals interact with the world. For many who engage in frequent conflict, the driving force is unresolved emotional trauma. These behaviours may serve as defence mechanisms, ways to protect oneself from perceived threats or relive familiar dynamics. This chapter explores how these patterns begin and how they can be unraveled with understanding and intentional change.

The Seeds of Conflict:

A Story of Childhood Trauma:

Imagine a boy named Marcus, raised in a household where yelling was the norm and silence was dangerous. His father, a man quick to anger, ruled with harsh words and heavy hands, while his mother withdrew, avoiding conflict at all costs. In this volatile environment, Marcus learned two things: conflict was inevitable, and the louder voice always won.

As Marcus grew older, the chaotic environment imprinted itself deep within his psyche. Moments of peace were rare, and any slight deviation in tone could be the spark for an explosive argument. Even as a child, Marcus would sense the storm brewing—his father's raised voice like thunder rumbling in the distance. His own body would tense, his heart pounding as if expecting lightning to strike at any moment. By the time he was a teenager, Marcus's world was one where aggression was survival.

Now an adult, Marcus finds himself in frequent arguments, both at work and at home. His default reaction to disagreement is aggressive— he shouts, pushes, and refuses to back down. Inside, it feels as though every disagreement threatens to unravel the fragile sense of control he clings to. His anger builds quickly, like a dam about to burst, each word or perceived slight adding pressure. The roots of his high-conflict behaviour are tied to the instability he experienced early in life, the echoes of his childhood chaos reverberating in his adult relationships.

Reflection Exercise:

Think about a recent conflict you encountered. What emotions came up for you during that moment? Were you reminded of an experience that might have influenced your reaction? Write down your thoughts to identify any connections between your past and present behaviour.

....
....
....

Learning by Example:

How Conflict Breeds Conflict.

Meet Angela. Growing up, her parents fought constantly—about money, chores, everything. There was never a sense of peace in her home. Over time, Angela came to believe that conflict was an inevitable part of relationships, something to endure rather than resolve. As a young girl, she would lie in bed, listening to her parents' voices rise and clash like swords. Each argument felt like a battle, one she could never escape.

As an adult, Angela brought this belief into her marriage. When small disagreements arose, she would escalate them, convinced that conflict needed to be fought out to be resolved. For her, every disagreement was a war zone where retreat was not an option. It was as if her childhood had taught her that conflict was a fire to be stoked, rather than something that could be gently extinguished.

Her husband, on the other hand, came from a family where problems were discussed calmly. He found Angela's approach overwhelming, retreating into silence or avoidance. This dynamic pushed them further apart—Angela saw his withdrawal as indifference, while he viewed her confrontations as irrational and exhausting. Their conflicting expectations of how to handle problems created a cycle of escalating tension, one where each partner felt misunderstood.

Reflection Prompt:

Think about your own approach to conflict. Do you tend to escalate disagreements or avoid them altogether? Where might you have learned these patterns—was it from your family, past relationships, or other experiences? Write down any insights you have.

....

....

....

....

Insecurity's Shadow: The Fear of Vulnerability.

James is a successful entrepreneur, confident in his professional life but deeply insecure in his personal relationships. Beneath his outward success lies a fear of rejection, an old wound that never fully healed. He often perceives innocent remarks from his wife or colleagues as personal attacks. A passing comment about his work or a suggestion from his wife feels like a threat, as if exposing a hidden weakness.

When James feels criticized, his instinct is to lash out—better to defend himself than risk being vulnerable. His fear of rejection, stemming from an insecure attachment in his childhood, has grown into a full-blown defence mechanism. He equates vulnerability with danger, constantly feeling like he is one misstep away from being exposed as unworthy. As a result, he pushes people away, creating a self-fulfilling prophecy of isolation.

Reflection Exercise:

Consider a recent disagreement where you felt personally attacked. What emotions were present for you? Was it fear, insecurity, or something else? Write down your thoughts and think about whether your reaction was a defence against feeling vulnerable.

....

....

....

....

The Impact of Personality Disorders:

The Struggles for Control.

Sarah's life has always felt like it is spiralling out of control. Diagnosed with borderline personality disorder (BPD), Sarah experiences intense emotional swings. Small frustrations quickly turn into overwhelming feelings of anger. Her emotions surge like a tidal wave, consuming everything in their path. Her fear of abandonment is ever present, a dark cloud that hangs over her interactions. Even the slightest hint of someone pulling away sends her into a panic, and her response is to lash out, desperate to regain control.

Unfortunately, these actions often push people further away. Her intense emotional responses and impulsive behaviour make it difficult for her to keep stable relationships. The more she tries to control, the more she feels abandoned, which only deepens her pain and fuels more high-conflict behaviour.

Simplified Explanation of BPD:

Borderline Personality Disorder (BPD) is a condition that can cause extreme emotional reactions and intense fear of abandonment, making it difficult to maintain stable relationships. If you would like to learn more, please refer to the glossary at the end of the book for further explanation.

Solutions for Breaking the Cycle of High Conflict Behaviour:

Self-awareness and reflection are the first steps in overcoming high conflict behaviour. Whether it stems from childhood trauma, learned patterns, or underlying insecurity, understanding the roots of these tendencies allows for growth. The following strategies can help in breaking the cycle:

Self-Awareness and Reflection:

Recognizing your emotional triggers is crucial. Tools like journaling, therapy, and self-reflection can help you identify patterns and understand their origins.

Emotional Regulation Techniques:

Learning how to regulate emotions in the heat of the moment is essential. Techniques like deep breathing, grounding exercises, and mindfulness can help calm your nervous system and create space before reacting impulsively.

Improved Communication Skills:

Many conflicts arise from miscommunication or poor habits. Practicing clear expression of needs, active listening, and engaging in non-defensive dialogue can dramatically reduce the intensity of conflicts.

Reframing Conflict:

Rather than viewing conflict as a battle, try to see it as an opportunity for growth. This perspective shift helps reduce the emotional charge associated with disagreements and promotes problem-solving over confrontation.

Therapeutic Support:

For those whose high-conflict behaviour is deeply rooted in trauma or personality disorders, therapy—such as cognitive-behavioural therapy (CBT) or dialectical behaviour therapy (DBT)—can provide the guidance needed to heal and develop healthier behaviours.

Exercise:

Reflect on the strategies mentioned above. Which one stands out as most relevant to your experiences? Commit to practicing one of these techniques, such as mindful breathing or active listening, the next time you face a conflict.

Breaking free from high-conflict patterns takes patience and dedication, but it is possible with the right mindset and support. Whether it involves acknowledging past wounds, learning new skills, or seeking professional help, each step forward brings individuals closer to a more peaceful, fulfilling life.

CHAPTER 1 WORKBOOK.

"Born from Chaos: The Roots of High-Conflict Behaviour"

Reflection Questions:

Reflect on your upbringing. Were conflicts frequent in your household? How were they handled?

....
....
....
....

What patterns of behaviour did you adopt from your parents or caretakers in relation to conflict?

....
....
....
....

How do you currently react when you feel challenged or criticized? What emotions come up for you?

....
....
....
....

Action Steps:

Identify Patterns:

Reflect on your recent conflicts. Write down 3-5 examples of arguments or disagreements you've had in the past month. What were the triggers? Was there a common theme (e.g., feeling unappreciated, misunderstood, or controlled)?

....

....

....

....

Recognize Emotional Triggers:

For each conflict listed above, ask yourself: What was the underlying emotion I felt? (e.g., fear, anger, frustration, insecurity) Write down the specific emotion for each conflict. Becoming aware of your emotional triggers is the first step to gaining control over your reactions.

....

....

....

....

Activity:

Family influence:

If an incident occurs with a family member write down how the family a member handled conflict. Reflect on how their approaches have influenced your own behaviour. How are you similar? How are you different?

Conflict Incident:

Date: ______________

Who was involved? ______________

What was the conflict about? ______________

Emotional Response:

What emotions did I feel during this conflict? (Check all that apply):

☐ Anger

☐ Frustration

☐ Fear

☐ Sadness

☐ Other: ____________

What triggered my emotional response?

____

How did I respond?

____

What was the outcome of the conflict?

____

Reflection:

Could I have handled it differently? If so, how?

What key takeaways did I gain from this conflict?

What emotional trigger or pattern did I notice?

Next Steps:

What will I do different Next time?

CHAPTER 1 Personal Journal

Born from Chaos –

The Roots of High-Conflict Behaviour.

Reflect on how your early experiences have shaped your current approach to conflict.

Journal Reflection Prompts:

What early childhood experiences influenced your current approach to conflict?

How do you typically respond to feelings of anger or frustration in your relationships?

What patterns have you noticed in your conflict behaviour, and what steps can you take to address them?

Next Steps: Based on your reflection, what action steps will you take to start addressing high-conflict behaviour?

Resources:

Recommended Reading:
The Drama of the Gifted Child by Alice Miller (to further understand how childhood experiences shape adult behaviour)

Recommended Videos:
TED Talk: *How Childhood Trauma Affects Health Across a Lifetime* by Nadine Burke Harris.

CHAPTER TWO. The Storm Within:

Emotional Intelligence and High-Conflict Personalities.

Conflict often begins within, sparked by unrecognized emotions and an inability to manage them effectively. Emotional intelligence—the ability to recognize, understand, and manage one's own emotions, as well as those of others—is crucial in navigating the choppy waters of conflict. For those lacking this skill set, the result can be like standing in a storm without a rudder, swept up in chaos of their own making. In this chapter, we explore how deficits in emotional intelligence fuel high-conflict behaviour and offer strategies to develop the emotional tools necessary for smoother interactions.

The Unseen Trigger:

Ben's Battle with His Emotions.

Ben is a high achiever, known for his sharp intellect and quick thinking. Yet, despite his professional success, his personal relationships have always been fraught with tension. At home, small disagreements with his partner quickly spiral into full-blown arguments. A simple request to take out the trash can trigger an outburst about how unappreciated he feels. At work, he clashes with colleagues, interpreting feedback as a personal attack.

Ben is unaware that his emotional reactions are automatic and impulsive. When he feels wronged, defensiveness overwhelms him like a tidal wave. Without taking a moment to think, he responds aggressively, driven by unprocessed emotions such as frustration, insecurity, or fear. His lack of self-reflection prevents him from understanding his feelings, leading to these quick, hostile outbursts that push others away.

Mindfulness Exercise:

The next time you feel emotionally triggered, try pausing for a few moments and taking five deep breaths. This moment of mindfulness can help create a space between your emotions and reaction, allowing you to respond with more awareness.

The Avalanche Effect:

Rachel's Overwhelming Responses.

Rachel has always been passionate, but her passion often spills into her emotional reactions, turning small conflicts into overwhelming experiences. When her husband doesn't text her back right away, she assumes he's upset with her. If her coworker gets a promotion, she feels a wave of envy so intense that it colours every interaction with them. Rachel's emotions, like a sudden avalanche, seem to cascade out of her control, burying her ability to think clearly under their weight.

In these moments, Rachel feels as though her emotions are running the show. She's often embarrassed by the intensity of her feelings but doesn't know how to stop them. Her outbursts have strained friendships, and at work, she's gained a reputation for being unpredictable.

Emotional Regulation Practice:

When emotions start to build, try progressive muscle relaxation—focus on tensing and then releasing each muscle group, from your toes up to your head. This technique can help ground you and regain control over your emotional state.

Misunderstanding Others:

The Ripple Effect of Low Empathy.

Jason prides himself on being a logical thinker, someone who deals with facts and reason. But when it comes to understanding other people's emotions, Jason is adrift. When his wife is upset, he responds with practical solutions, often dismissing the feelings behind her concerns. At work, he brushes off colleagues' frustrations as irrational, believing they should focus solely on the tasks at hand.

Jason's lack of empathy creates emotional distance between him and others. He doesn't realize that his logical responses, while well intended, are often invalidating, leaving his wife and coworkers feeling unheard and disconnected. His relationships suffer, not because he's uncaring, but because he lacks the emotional awareness to recognize that emotional support can be just as important as problem-solving.

Empathy Development Activity:

Practice active listening in your next conversation—focus entirely on what the other person is saying without interrupting or offering solutions. Summarize their words back to them to ensure understanding before responding.

The Quick Temper:

David's Struggle with Impulse Control.

David is the life of the party, always quick with a joke or a story. But his impulsive nature, which makes him fun in casual settings, becomes a problem when things get serious. In arguments, David's temper flares quickly. He says hurtful things without thinking, blurting out words he instantly regrets. His quick temper has cost him friendships, strained his romantic relationships, and even jeopardized his career.

David knows he has a problem with impulsivity, but he feels powerless to stop it. His emotions seem to come out of nowhere, like a fire igniting in an instant, consuming his better judgment before he even has a chance to act thoughtfully.

Pause Technique:

When you feel your temper rising, count to ten before responding. This brief pause can help shift you from a reactive state to a more thoughtful, controlled response.

Building Emotional Intelligence: Solutions for Personal Growth

Self-Awareness:
Regularly check in with your emotions—through journaling or using an emotion-tracking app—to recognize patterns and triggers. This increased awareness lays the groundwork for making positive changes.

Mindfulness and Emotional Regulation:

Practices like meditation, deep breathing, or yoga can calm your nervous system and reduce emotional reactions. These exercises create a space between feeling and action, allowing you to respond more thoughtfully.

Empathy Development:

Strengthening empathy begins with active listening and trying to understand others' feelings. Exercises like imagining how others feel or reflecting on personal experiences of vulnerability can build this skill.

Effective Communication:

Learning to communicate emotions clearly can prevent misunderstandings. Using "I" statements (e.g., "I feel frustrated when...") instead of blaming others fosters a more productive dialogue.

Therapeutic Support:

If emotional regulation or empathy development feels challenging, therapy can provide valuable tools for growth.

CHAPTER 2 Workbook.

Reflection Questions:

How aware are you of your emotions in the heat of a conflict? Are you able to label them as they arise?

....
....
....

When others are upset, how do you typically respond? Do you listen, or do you immediately offer advice or defend your point of view?

....
....
....

Do you often feel overwhelmed by your emotions? How do you cope when that happens?

....
....
....

Action Steps:

Practice Mindful Listening:

The next time you're in a disagreement, commit to practicing mindful listening. Focus entirely on what the other person is saying without interrupting or preparing your counter argument.

Afterward, write down how the conversation felt different. Did you gain new insights? Did the other person seem more receptive?

....

....

....

Label Your Emotions:

Throughout the day, take moments to pause and check in with yourself. Use an emotion wheel (easily found online) to identify what you're feeling in specific moments. Write down the primary emotions you experience in a journal for one week.

....

....

....

Activity:

Emotion Journal:

For the next five days, keep an "emotion journal" where you track the emotions you feel during moments of conflict or stress. Use specific language to describe your emotions (e.g., instead of just "angry," you could write "frustrated" or "resentful"). At the end of each day, reflect on how labelling these emotions helped you become more aware of your reactions.

CHAPTER 2 Personal Journal

The Storm Within:

Emotional Intelligence and High-Conflict Personalities.

Reflect on your awareness of emotions during conflict and how you can improve your emotional intelligence.

Journal Reflection Prompts:

How aware are you of your emotions during conflict?

When others express frustration or anger, how do you typically respond?

What can you do to pause and manage your emotions before responding in conflict?

Next Steps:

Identify one emotional regulation technique (e.g., breathing, pausing) and how you will implement it.

Resources:

Recommended App:
Mood-Meter (an app for tracking emotions).

Recommended Reading:
Emotional Intelligence 2.0 by Travis Bradberry and Jean Greaves.

CHAPTER THREE. Defending the Fortress:

Insecurity and the Fear Behind Conflict:

Underneath the surface of high-conflict behaviour often lies a deeprooted fear of vulnerability. For many, confrontation is not an expression of strength but a shield against the fear of rejection, failure, or inadequacy. Insecurity silently fuels the flames of conflict, turning small disagreements into fierce battles as individuals try to defend their fragile sense of self. This chapter explores how insecurity triggers conflict and offers paths to build inner security and healthier, more resilient relationships.

The Armor of Aggression: A Story of Self-Protection.

Carmen had always been quick to defend herself. Whether it was a passing comment from a coworker or a disagreement with her partner, she often felt attacked, even when no harm was intended. One evening, her partner casually mentioned how she had forgotten to pick up milk on her way home—a simple, everyday oversight. But for Carmen, it felt like an accusation of failure.

"I can't believe you're blaming me for this! I have so much on my plate already!" she fired back, her voice rising with frustration. Her partner, taken aback, hadn't meant it as a criticism, but Carmen's response had escalated the situation into a heated argument.

Deep down, Carmen's quick defence wasn't about the milk at all. It was her insecurity speaking, her inner voice whispering that she wasn't good enough. She feared that if she wasn't perfect, she would be judged or worse, abandoned. In her mind, every criticism—even small ones—was a threat to her self-worth, so she built a wall of aggression to protect herself.

Reflection Exercise:

Think about a recent disagreement where you reacted defensively. Was it really about the issue at hand, or was it rooted in a deeper insecurity? Write down your thoughts and explore if your reaction was protecting something vulnerable within you.

....

....

....

The Fear of Rejection: Hidden Beneath Criticism.

Jack had always been the type to criticize those around him. He picked apart his wife's cooking, his kids' school projects, and even his friends' career choices. On the surface, it seemed like Jack was simply demanding high standards, but underneath lay a very different truth: Jack was terrified of rejection. He believed that if he wasn't perfect, if his family didn't live up to certain standards, they would all be judged— and by extension, so would he.

When his wife confronted him about his constant criticism, Jack doubled down. "I'm just trying to help you be better!" he exclaimed, his voice tight with frustration. But what Jack couldn't see was that his critical nature was pushing his loved ones away, creating the very isolation and rejection he feared most.

Exercise:

The next time you feel the urge to criticize, try to replace the critical thought with a supportive one. For example, instead of pointing out a flaw, acknowledge something positive.

CHAPTER 3 Workbook.

"Defending the Fortress:

Insecurity and the Fear Behind Conflict".

Reflection Questions:

Think about the last time you felt defensive during a conflict. What fear or insecurity may have been driving that reaction?

....

....

....

Do you find yourself needing to "win" an argument to feel validated? Why do you think that is?

....

....

....

In what ways do you seek control over situations or people? How does that affect your relationships?

....

....

....

Action Steps:

Challenge Negative Beliefs:
Write down a list of beliefs you hold about yourself that may contribute to insecurity. For example, "If I'm wrong, people will think I'm incompetent" or "I need to be perfect to be accepted." Next to each

belief, write a rational counterstatement that challenges it (e.g., "It's okay to make mistakes; people respect honesty").

....
....
....

Vulnerability Practice:
In your next conversation, practice sharing a small vulnerability. This could be as simple as admitting you don't know the answer to something or sharing an honest feeling. Afterward, reflect on how the other person responded. Did it create connection or conflict?

....
....
....

Activity:

Breaking the Fear Cycle:
Identify one fear that frequently shows up in your conflicts (e.g., fear of failure, fear of rejection). Create a plan for how you will face this fear head-on the next time it arises. For example, if you fear rejection, practice affirming your worth to yourself before entering a difficult conversation.

....
....
....

CHAPTER 3 Personal Journal:

Defending the Fortress.

Insecurity and the Fear Behind Conflict:

Explore the insecurities that may drive your conflict responses and how to work through them.

What insecurities Journal Reflection Prompts:

drive your reactions during conflict?

Do you feel the need to "win" conflicts to validate yourself? Why?

What steps can you take to build self-confidence and reduce your defensiveness?

Next Steps: Write down one insecurity or fear you will confront and how you plan to address it in future conflicts.

CHAPTER FOUR. Escaping the Cycle:

The Role of Personality Disorders in High Conflict Behaviour:

Not all conflicts are created equal. Some are born from misunderstandings, insecurities, or stress, but others are more deeply rooted in the way people see the world and interact with it. Personality disorders—long-term patterns of thinking, feeling, and behaving—can make conflicts feel not only more intense but also more frequent and unmanageable. These disorders often lead to behaviour patterns where emotional chaos, manipulation, and confrontation dominate. In this chapter, we'll dive into how certain personality disorders fuel high conflict behaviour and explore some practical ways forward— both for the individuals experiencing these disorders and for those affected by them.

The Battle of Identity:

Living with Borderline Personality Disorder (BPD)

Lydia's emotions ran her life. One moment, she felt completely adored by her partner, like she was the center of his world. But if he was a few minutes late coming home or forgot to call, her emotions flipped like a switch. Suddenly, Lydia felt abandoned, unlovable, and consumed by rage. Her partner, Paul, had grown used to her emotional rollercoasters, but each outburst left him feeling more distant, unsure how to navigate the constant shift between affection and fury.

For Lydia, every conflict felt like a battle for survival. With borderline personality disorder (BPD), her fear of abandonment was so intense that she often lashed out before even processing her feelings. Her world was black-and-white—either everything was perfect, or it was a disaster. In that space, conflicts erupted over things that, to others, might seem insignificant.

Reflection Prompt:

When you find yourself reacting intensely to a situation, pause and ask yourself if the reaction matches the situation. Is it about what's happening now, or is it tied to a past fear or experience?

The Narcissist's Mirror:

Self-Absorption and Conflict

Alex seemed like the perfect partner at first. He was charming, confident, and ambitious—everything Sarah thought she wanted. But after a while, Sarah noticed something troubling. Anytime she tried to talk about her own feelings or concerns, Alex would shift the focus back to himself. If she shared an achievement, Alex would one-up her. And when they argued, he never took responsibility. It was always someone else's fault—never his.

Alex displayed traits of narcissistic personality disorder (NPD), where the need for admiration and validation overshadowed everything else. For people like Alex, conflicts arise because they can't tolerate criticism or admit to any flaws. In their world, they must be the best, the smartest, and the most successful, so any perceived threat to that image leads to defensiveness, manipulation, or even emotional abuse.

Empathy Development Activity:

Practice perspective-taking by imagining how someone else might feel in a situation before responding. This can help shift your focus from yourself to the other person's experience.

CHAPTER 4 WORKBOOK.

"Escaping the Cycle: The Role of Personality Disorders in High Conflict behaviour"

Reflection Questions:

Do you recognize any traits of personality disorders (e.g., narcissism, borderline, or obsessive-compulsive tendencies) in yourself or someone you know? How have these traits affected your relationships?

....
....
....

When faced with someone who has a high-conflict personality, do you tend to enable their behaviour or set boundaries?

....
....
....

Action Steps:

Understanding Personality Disorders:

Research one personality disorder that resonates with what you've experienced (whether in yourself or a loved one). Write a summary of how this disorder manifests in relationships and what strategies are most effective for managing it.

....

....

....

Set Clear Boundaries:
Identify one high-conflict relationship in your life. Write down specific boundaries you can set to protect your emotional well-being. This could include time limits on arguments, agreeing not to engage in conversations when voices are raised, or stating that you will not tolerate certain behaviours.

Activity:

Boundary Setting Script:
Draft a script for setting boundaries in a conflict situation.
Use assertive language, such as, "I value our relationship, but I need to step away when the conversation becomes disrespectful." Practice delivering this script with confidence.

Resources:

Recommended Reading:
Stop Walking on Eggshells by Paul Mason and Randi Kreger (for understanding borderline personality disorder).

Recommended Article:
How to Set Boundaries with Narcissists on Psychology Today.

CHAPETR 4 Personal Journal:

Escaping the Cycle – The Role of Personality Disorders in High Conflict Behaviour:

Consider how personality traits or disorders may affect your relationships and how to manage them.

Journal Reflection Prompts:

Do you recognize any high-conflict personality traits in yourself or others?

How do these behaviours impact your relationships?

What boundaries can you set to protect your emotional wellbeing in high-conflict relationships?

Next Steps: Write down one boundary you will set in a high conflict relationship and how you will communicate it.

CHAPTER FIVE. Breaking the Chains:

Solutions for Managing High-Conflict Personalities:

High-conflict personalities often create emotional storms, but like any storm, they can be navigated and eventually calmed. While these deeply ingrained behaviour patterns drive conflict, they are not unchangeable. This chapter focuses on practical solutions—tools and strategies that can help individuals break free from the cycle of conflict. These approaches work not only for those who exhibit high conflict tendencies but also for those who live or work alongside them.

The Endless Debate: Learning to Step Back.

James and Rachel's marriage was filled with constant debates. Every conversation felt like a contest—a power struggle where neither could back down. Whether they were discussing what movie to watch or how to discipline their children, every issue escalated into a full-blown argument. James, being a lawyer, was used to winning arguments with logic, while Rachel, driven by her emotions, refused to concede ground.

The problem wasn't the topics themselves; it was their inability to let go. Both felt the need to be right, and being right became more important than peace in their home. Even the smallest disagreements felt monumental, creating an atmosphere of constant tension.

Reflection Prompt:

Think about a recent disagreement you had. Was it truly about the issue, or was it more about feeling the need to win? Write down what was at stake for you emotionally. Could letting go have changed the outcome?

Pause and Reflect Exercise:

Before engaging in an argument, take a moment to pause and ask yourself, "Is this worth a fight?" This simple question can help you gain perspective and choose a more peaceful approach.

The Walls We Build:

Addressing Emotional Withdrawal.

For years, Adam relied on silence as a defence mechanism. When conflict arose with his wife, Emily, he would retreat into himself, shutting down emotionally. Emily, on the other hand, craved communication and would push harder to get Adam to talk, which only made him withdraw further. It became a painful cycle—Emily felt abandoned, and Adam felt overwhelmed.

Adam's withdrawal wasn't about indifference; it was about fear. Growing up in a family where emotions were rarely discussed, he learned to cope by building emotional walls, believing silence was safer than engaging in a potential argument.

Intentional Engagement Practice:

Schedule specific times for open communication with a loved one, where both parties can express feelings in a safe, calm environment. Planning these conversations can make it easier for someone who struggles with emotional withdrawal to engage.

Reflection Exercise:

The next time you feel the urge to withdraw, pause and identify what you're feeling. Is it fear, discomfort, or something else? Write down your thoughts to better understand what you're protecting yourself from.

The Critic:

Transforming Negative Communication.

Jennifer was the critic in her marriage, though she didn't see it that way. She loved her husband, Tom, but her need for control often manifested as constant criticism. If Tom didn't do the dishes "right" or made a mistake with the budget, Jennifer would point it out, thinking she was helping him improve. But to Tom, it felt like a never-ending stream of judgment, which gradually eroded his self-confidence.

Tom, in response, began withdrawing from tasks altogether. Nothing he did seemed good enough, which created a cycle of frustration and emotional distance between them.

Positive Reinforcement Activity:

The next time you feel the urge to criticize, try replacing the criticism with positive reinforcement. For example, acknowledge something your partner did well before bringing up areas for improvement. This can help create a more supportive environment.

Reflection Prompt:

Consider how often you offer praise compared to criticism in your relationships. Do you find yourself focusing more on flaws than on strengths? Write down three things you appreciate about your loved one to shift your perspective.

....

The Need for Control:

Letting Go of Perfection.

Charles built his life around control. As an engineer, he thrived on structure, and his home reflected that same need for order. His wife, Laura, admired his attention to detail, but over time, Charles's need for control became overwhelming. Laura, who was more spontaneous and laid-back, felt stifled by his rigid routines and constant need for things to be done in a particular way.

For Charles, control wasn't just about order; it was a way to manage his anxiety. Growing up in a chaotic household, he'd learned to create order to feel safe. But in his marriage, this need for perfection created tension, leaving Laura feeling as though there was no room for flexibility or spontaneity.

Intentional Imperfection Exercise:

Allow small deviations from your usual routines and sit with the discomfort that may arise. For example, let a loved one load the dishwasher their way or decide on plans without intervening. This practice can help reduce the anxiety associated with letting go of control.

CHAPTER 5 WORKBOOK:

"Breaking the Chains: Solutions for Managing High- Conflict **Personalities"**

Reflection Questions:

How comfortable are you with managing your own emotions during conflict?

....
....
....

When someone close to you is engaging in high-conflict behaviour, how do you typically respond? What could you do differently?

....
....
....

Action Steps:

Implement Emotional Regulation Techniques:

Practice one emotional regulation technique, such as deep breathing or the 10-second rule, in your next conflict situation. Write down the effect it had on your ability to stay calm and respond thoughtfully.

....
....

....

Communicate with Clarity:

In your next difficult conversation, practice using "I" statements instead of "“You” r" statements (e.g., "I feel hurt when..." instead of "You always..."). Reflect afterward on how this approach changed the tone of the conversation.

....
....
....

Activity:

Conflict Role-Play:
Find a trusted friend or family member and role-play a conflict situation. Practice staying calm, using "I" statements, and setting boundaries. After the role-play, discuss what worked and what could be improved.

Resources:

Recommended Reading:
Crucial Conversations by Kerry Patterson, Joseph Grenny, and Ron McMillan (for mastering difficult conversations).

Recommended Videos:
YouTube: *How to Manage Emotional Triggers in Conflict* by The School of Life.

CHAPTER 5 Personal Journal:

Breaking the Chains – Solutions for Managing High- Conflict Personalities:

Find practical solutions for managing conflict effectively.

Journal Reflection Prompts:

How have you managed emotions in past conflict situations?

What emotional regulation techniques will you use in future conflicts?

How will setting clearer boundaries help you navigate high-conflict personalities?

Next Steps: Choose one strategy to practice in your next conflict and write about how you plan to use it.

CHAPTER SIX. Healing Through Understanding:

Helping High-Conflict Loved Ones:

When someone we love displays high-conflict behaviour, it can feel like walking on thin ice, never knowing when it might crack beneath us. The emotional toll is heavy, and the path forward may seem unclear. However, there is hope. In this chapter, we explore how understanding, patience, and firm boundaries can help those who live with high-conflict personalities foster healthier, more harmonious relationships. It's not about fixing others but about supporting them while protecting your own well-being.

The Unspoken Struggle:

Supporting Without Rescuing.

Clara loved her brother, Aaron, but his temper was exhausting. No matter how small the issue, Aaron always found a way to turn it into a full-blown argument. Over time, Clara found herself walking on eggshells, constantly trying to keep the peace.

What Clara didn't realize was that her constant rescuing was feeding Aaron's behaviour. By stepping in every time, he became upset, Clara was unintentionally reinforcing the idea that Aaron didn't have to manage his emotions. As much as she loved her brother, Clara had to acknowledge that she couldn't save him from his own anger.

Reflection Prompt:

Think of a time when you "rescued" someone in a conflict. How did it affect the situation in the long run? Write down how stepping back could have created a different outcome.

Boundary-Setting Practice:

The next time a loved one reacts with anger or conflict, set a clear boundary. For example, say, "I'll continue this conversation when we can both speak calmly." This approach allows space for growth without enabling the behaviour.

The Partner's Dilemma: Loving While Standing Firm.

Michael had fallen in love with Laura's passionate nature. She was vibrant, opinionated, and always ready to fight for what she believed in. But as their relationship deepened, Michael started to realize that Laura's passion often crossed into conflict. Small decisions would turn into fiery arguments, and Michael felt drained.

At first, Michael thought that giving in to Laura's demands would keep the peace, but the more he conceded, the more control she exerted. It became clear that love alone wasn't enough to heal their relationship—he needed to protect his own emotional health too.

Reflection Exercise:

Write down three ways you can maintain boundaries in your relationship without withdrawing emotionally. Consider how setting these boundaries can create a healthier dynamic.

....

....

....

....

Compassionate Boundary Setting:

Practice saying, “I care about our relationship, but I need us to have this conversation when we’re both calm.” This shows care while also protecting your well-being.

CHAPTER 6 Workbook.

"Healing Through Understanding: Helping High-Conflict Loved Ones"

Reflection Questions:

Are you currently in a relationship where you feel you are constantly managing the other person's emotions? How does this affect your mental and emotional health?

How comfortable are you with setting and maintaining boundaries with high conflict loved ones?

....
....
....

Action Steps:

Identify Enabling Behaviours:
Reflect on ways you may have enabled a high conflict loved one's behaviour. Write down specific instances where you took on the role of emotional caretaker or peacemaker. What could you do differently in the future?

....
....

……………………………………………………………………………………………

Self-Care Plan:

Create a self-care plan for yourself. Include activities and practices that help you recharge emotionally (e.g., therapy, journaling, meditation). Commit to prioritizing these activities, even when conflicts arise.

Activity:

Boundary Reflection:
Think of a recent instance where you set a boundary with a high conflict loved one. Write down how it made you feel and how the other person reacted. Reflect on what worked and what challenges you faced in enforcing that boundary.

……………………………………………………………………………………………
……………………………………………………………………………………………
……………………………………………………………………………………………

Resources.

Recommended Read:

Book: *"Boundaries: When to Say Yes, How to Say No to Take Control of Your Life"* by Dr. Henry Cloud & Dr. John Townsend.

Recommended Video:

Video: *"How to Deal with Difficult People and Set Boundaries"* by Dr. Ramani Durvasula.

CHAPTER 6 Personal Journal:

Healing Through Understanding – Helping High-Conflict Loved Ones.

Reflect on how you manage relationships with high conflict loved ones and protect your emotional well-being.

Journal Reflection Prompts:

Have you enabled a high conflict loved one's behaviour? How?

What boundaries can you set to manage their behaviour and protect yourself?

What self-care strategies can you implement to manage stress from these relationships?

Next Steps:

Write a self-care plan to help manage stress from high-conflict relationships.

CHAPTER SEVEN. Finding Balance.

Supporting Growth Without Enabling.

When living with or loving a high-conflict individual, the line between support and enabling can blur. On one side lies compassion, the desire to help, and the hope for improvement. On the other side, there's the risk of reinforcing unhealthy behaviour by constantly stepping in to fix or pacify. The key lies in recognizing when your help stops being beneficial and starts fuelling the very behaviour you wish to change. This chapter explores how to support someone's growth without becoming an enabler and how to foster independence amid emotional chaos.

The Trap of Enabling.

In her marriage to Derek, Nina had long taken on the role of peacemaker. Derek was easily triggered, often reacting angrily to minor inconveniences—a delayed bill payment, an unplanned visit from relatives, or even a change in dinner plans. Each time his anger rose, Nina stepped in, smoothing things over with gentle words or quietly handling the situation. Over time, Nina felt overwhelmed and resentful.

What Nina did not realize was that by constantly calming Derek, she was preventing him from learning how to manage his emotions. She was enabling his behaviour by shielding him from the consequences of his outbursts. The more she stepped in, the more Derek's behaviour escalated.

Reflection Prompt:

Think of a time when you stepped in to "fix" a situation for someone else. Did it change their behaviour long-term, or did it become a pattern?

Write down ways you can allow others to take responsibility for their actions.

Exercise for Practicing Detachment:

The next time you're tempted to step in, take a moment to pause. Ask yourself, "Am I helping or enabling?" Let the other person experience the natural consequences of their actions.

Encouraging Accountability:

Enabling often happens in subtle ways—a sigh of resignation here, a placating comment there. But real growth requires accountability, and accountability requires standing firm, even when it feels uncomfortable. When someone avoids the natural consequences of their actions, they miss the opportunity to learn and grow. Whether in a romantic partnership, a friendship, or a family relationship, fostering personal accountability is a cornerstone of helping, not enabling.

Accountability Practice:

Encourage loved ones to take responsibility for their emotions and actions by saying, "I'm here to support you, but I need you to take the first step." This allows space for growth without taking away their agency.

CHAPTER 7 Workbook.

Finding Balance.

Supporting Growth Without Enabling.

Reflection Questions:

Do you often feel responsible for managing other people's emotions in high-conflict situations? How does this affect your emotional wellbeing?

....
....
....

Can you identify moments where you enabled someone's high-conflict behaviour instead of supporting their growth? What happened?

....
....
....

What changes could you make to foster personal responsibility in others without taking on their emotional burdens?

....
....
....
....

Action Steps:

Step Back:

Identify one relationship in which you often feel responsible for the other person's emotions. Write down specific boundaries you can implement to allow them to take responsibility for their emotional state, while also protecting your own well-being.

....
....
....
....

Encourage Responsibility:

The next time you feel tempted to step in and fix a high-conflict situation, pause, and reflect on whether you are helping or enabling. Practice allowing the other person to manage their emotions without your intervention.

....
....
....

Activity: Support vs. Enable.

Make a list of behaviours you have engaged in that may be enabling high-conflict personalities (e.g., placating them, always giving in to avoid arguments). In a separate column, write down healthier alternatives that encourage their growth instead of relying on you to solve their problems.

....
....
....
....

Resources:

Recommended Reading:

"Stop Caretaking the Borderline or Narcissist" by Margalis Fjelstad.

Recommended Video:

"How to Stop Enabling in Relationships" on YouTube by The Holistic Psychologist.

CHAPTER 7 Personal Journal:

Finding Balance – Supporting Growth Without Enabling:

Reflect on the balance between supporting someone and enabling high conflict behaviour.

Journal Reflection Prompts:

Do you feel the need to "fix" other people's emotions or conflicts?

How can you step back and encourage accountability instead of enabling?

What makes you detach with compassion?

Next Steps: Practice detaching from emotional over-involvement and write about your experience.

CHAPTER EIGHT. Breaking Free:

How High-Conflict Individuals Can Change:

For those who struggle with high-conflict tendencies, it can feel as if chaos and argument are inevitable companions. However, change is possible, but it requires a willingness to confront painful truths and take deliberate action. This chapter delves into the internal work necessary to break free from destructive patterns and how to begin the journey toward healthier, more peaceful relationships.

Recognizing the Role of Fear.

At the core of most high-conflict behaviour lies fear. Whether it's fear of rejection, failure, or vulnerability, this emotional undercurrent drives reactions that often seem disproportionate to the situation. For many, anger becomes a shield against these deep-seated fears. Understanding this emotional dynamic is the first step toward change.

Take the case of Jonathan, a successful entrepreneur who thrived on control. At work, his authoritative and unyielding style often led to clashes with employees. At home, this need for control manifested in frequent arguments with his wife, Emily. If plans changed without his input or if Emily disagreed with him on a decision, Jonathan's temper flared. For years, he justified his behaviour as being a man who knew what he wanted. But beneath the surface, Jonathan's anger stemmed from a fear of powerlessness—something he had never acknowledged.

Reflection Prompt:

Think about a recent argument or conflict you experienced. Was there a deeper fear driving your reaction? Was it fear of losing control, being judged, or feeling vulnerable? Write down your thoughts and explore what you were afraid of.

Fear Exploration Exercise:

The next time you feel anger rising, pause and ask yourself, "What am I afraid of in this moment?" Identifying the underlying fear can help shift your perspective and guide you toward a more thoughtful response.

Developing Emotional Intelligence:

High-conflict behaviour often stems from an inability to manage emotions effectively. Learning to recognize triggers, pause before reacting, and regulate emotional responses is critical for long-term change. While this process can be difficult, it is the foundation of emotional intelligence—the key to breaking free from conflict-driven relationships.

Mindfulness Practice:

Incorporate a daily mindfulness routine, even for just five minutes. Close your eyes, take deep breaths and focus, observe any thoughts or emotions that arise without judgment. This practice can build awareness and improve your ability to pause before reacting.

Taking Responsibility:

Change begins when you take responsibility for your role in conflicts. This means acknowledging that while you cannot control others, you can control how you respond. It also means letting go of blame and focusing on what you can change within yourself.

Accountability Exercise:

Write down a recent conflict and identify what you could have done differently. What steps can you take to respond differently in similar situations in the future? This exercise encourages personal accountability and proactive behaviour change.

....
....
....
....

CHAPTER 8 Workbook.

Breaking Free:

How High-Conflict Individuals Can Change.

Reflection Questions:

What fears or emotional triggers contribute to your high conflict behaviour? How have these fears influenced your reactions?

....
....
....
....

What areas of your life have suffered because of unresolved conflict or emotional reactions?

....
....
....
....

What small steps can you take to change your high conflict behaviour, starting today?

....
....
....

....

Action Steps:

Identity Triggers:

Reflect on a recent conflict you were involved in. Write down the specific emotional triggers you experienced (e.g., feeling disrespected, fear of losing control). Next, write how you might respond differently the next time that trigger arises.

....
....
....
....

Pause Before Reacting:
Commit to pausing and counting to ten the next time you feel emotionally charged during a conflict. Write down the effect it has on your ability to respond thoughtfully rather than react impulsively.

....
....
....
....

Activity: Breaking Old Patterns:

For one week, keep track of any high-conflict interactions you experience. Each evening, reflect on the conflicts and note how you responded, what triggered you, and whether you were able to pause and respond differently. Reflect on any progress made by the end of the week.
....
....

....

....

Resources:

Recommended Reading:
"Emotional Agility" by Susan David.
Recommended Podcast:
"Unlocking Us" by Brené Brown (episodes on emotional triggers and vulnerability).

CHATER 8 Personal Journal:

Breaking Free:

How High-Conflict Individuals Can Change.

Explore your own ability for change and develop strategies to break free from conflict patterns.

Journal Reflection Prompts:

What fears drive your high-conflict reactions?

How can you confront these fears and change your responses?

What will be your first step in breaking free from high-conflict behaviour?

Next Steps: Write down one fear you will challenge in your next conflict situation and how you will handle it.

CHAPTER NINE. Rebuilding Relationships:

Transforming Conflict into Connection:

Once high-conflict behaviour begins to change, the next step is rebuilding the relationships affected by it. Transformation isn't just about stopping arguments; it's about cultivating new patterns of communication, trust, and respect. In this chapter, we explore how individuals can rebuild relationships after conflict and foster deeper connections beyond the absence of anger.

The Aftermath of Change:

After years of volatile interactions, the absence of conflict can feel disorienting. It's not uncommon for individuals and couples to experience a sense of emptiness or uncertainty when the habitual fighting stops. This is a pivotal moment—an opportunity to replace negative patterns with positive ones, to fill the space once occupied by tension with understanding and connection.

Sarah and Daniel had been married for nearly a decade when they finally sought help with their constant arguments. For years, their relationship had been a battleground, with every disagreement escalating into a shouting match. But after months of therapy and learning new communication techniques, the fights gradually ceased. Yet, when the noise stopped, Sarah and Daniel found themselves struggling to reconnect. The absence of conflict revealed how much distance had grown between them.

Reflection Exercise:

Think about a relationship in your life where conflict has decreased. How have your interactions changed since then? Write down how you feel about the silence or calm that has replaced the conflict. Are there new ways you can fill that space with connection?

Building Intimacy Activity:

Plan a time to connect with your partner or loved one outside of the usual routines. Whether it's a walk, a shared hobby, or an open conversation about dreams and goals, making time for intentional, positive interactions can strengthen the bond.

Cultivating Empathy and Trust.

At the heart of every successful relationship is empathy—the ability to understand and share the feelings of another. For individuals recovering from high-conflict behaviour, cultivating empathy can be a powerful tool in rebuilding relationships. Empathy allows you to step out of your own perspective and see the world through your loved one's eyes, fostering deeper trust and connection.

Empathy Exercise:

During your next interaction, practice active listening. Focus entirely on the other person's words without thinking about your response. Reflect what they've said to show understanding. This builds empathy and demonstrates your commitment to meaningful dialogue.

Building a Future Together.

Rebuilding after conflict isn't a one-time fix; it's an ongoing process that requires attention and care. But with each step forward, relationships can evolve into something stronger, more resilient, and filled with genuine connection. As you move through this process, remember that setbacks are natural, but each moment of understanding brings you closer to the relationship you've always wanted.

Commitment to Growth:

Write down a few goals for your relationships, such as practicing empathy, creating open communication times, or showing appreciation. Revisiting these goals regularly can help maintain progress and keep you focused on the positive changes you are working toward.

CHAPTER 9 Workbook.

Rebuilding Relationships.

Transforming Conflict into Connection.

Reflection Questions:

What steps can you take to repair relationships that has been damaged by high-conflict behaviour?

....

....

....

....

How can you communicate more effectively to foster understanding and connection in your relationships?

....

....

....

....

In what ways can you show empathy during conflicts to strengthen your relationships?

....

....

....

....

Action Steps:

Apologize with Intention:

Identify one relationship that has been damaged by conflict. Write down a plan to reach out, apologize, and take responsibility for your actions. Reflect on how you can use this moment to rebuild trust.

Active Listening Practice:
The next time you are in a difficult conversation, practice active listening. Focus entirely on the other person's perspective before responding. Write down how these changes the tone of the conversation and what insights you gained.

....
....
....
....

Activity:

Empathy in Conflict.

Think of a recent conflict where you failed to empathize with the other person. Write down how you could have approached the situation with more empathy, and how you believe this would have impacted the outcome. Practice applying this empathy in future interactions.

....
....
....
....

Resources:

Recommended Reading:
"The Seven Principles for Making Marriage Work" by John Gottman
Recommended Video:
"TEDx Talk: How Empathy Fuels Connection" by Brené Brown

CHAPTER 9 Personal Journal:

Rebuilding Relationships:

Transforming Conflict into Connection.

Reflect on how to rebuild trust and strengthen relationships after conflict.

Journal Reflection Prompts:

What steps will you take to rebuild trust in a relationship affected by conflict?

____

____

____

How can empathy improve communication and strengthen your connections?

____

____

____

What does a peaceful, conflict-free relationship look like to you?

____

____

____

Next Steps:

TAMING THE STORM

Write down one action you will take this week to rebuild a strained relationship.

Conflict Journal Section.

Use this section to track specific incidents of conflict, reflect on your emotional responses, and find patterns in your behaviour. This ongoing process will help you improve your conflict management skills and check your emotional growth over time.

Conflict Incident:

Continue your journey of conflict management.

Date: ________________

Who was involved? ________________ What was the conflict about?

____

Emotional Response:

What emotions did I feel during this conflict? (Check all that apply):

☐ Anger

☐ Frustration

☐ Fear

☐ Sadness

☐ Other: _____________

What triggered my emotional response?

How did I respond?

What was the outcome of the conflict?

Reflection:

Could I have handled it differently? If so, how?

What key takeaways did I gain from this conflict?

What emotional trigger or pattern did I notice?

Next Steps:

What will I do differently next time?

Conflict Incident:

Continue your journey of conflict management.

Date: _______________

Who was involved? _______________

What was the conflict about? _______________

Emotional Response:

What emotions did I feel during this conflict?

(Check all that apply):

☐ Anger.

☐ Frustration.

☐ Fear.

☐ Sadness.

☐ Other: ____________

What triggered my emotional response?

How did I respond?

What was the outcome of the conflict?

Reflection:

Could I have handled it differently? If so, how?

What key takeaways did I gain from this conflict?

What emotional trigger or pattern did I notice?

Next Steps:

What will I do differently next time?

Conflict Incident:

Continue your journey of conflict management.

Date: _______________

Who was involved? ______________

What was the conflict about? _______________

Emotional Response:

What emotions did I feel during this conflict? (Check all that apply):

☐ Anger.

☐ Frustration.

☐ Fear.

☐ Sadness.

☐ Other: ____________

What triggered my emotional response?

How did I respond?

What was the outcome of the conflict?

Reflection:

Could I have handled it differently? If so, how?

What key takeaways did I gain from this conflict?

What emotional trigger or pattern did I notice?

Next Steps:

What will I do differently next time?

Conflict Incident:

Continue your journey of conflict management.

Date: ________________

Who was involved? _______________

What was the conflict about? ________________

Emotional Response:

What emotions did I feel during this conflict? (Check all that apply):

☐ Anger.

☐ Frustration.

☐ Fear.

☐ Sadness.

☐ Other: _____________

What triggered my emotional response?

How did I respond?

What was the outcome of the conflict?

Reflection:

Could I have handled it differently? If so, how?

What key takeaways did I gain from this conflict?

What emotional trigger or pattern did I notice?

Next Steps:

What will I do differently next time?

Continue your journey.

Your personal journey of growth does not stop when you finish ***Taming the Storm***. Use this space to continue reflecting on your progress, writing down your goals, and documenting your ongoing emotional growth. **These blank pages are for you to freely explore any thoughts, ideas, or experiences that arise as you continue to apply the lessons from this book in your everyday life.**

Personal Growth Journal:

Date: ________________

____

____

____

____

____

Ongoing Reflections:
Date: ________________

____

____

____

____

____

Emotional Milestones:
Date: ________________

____

____

____

____

____

This journal is your safe space for continuous self-reflection and emotional growth. As you move forward, keep revisiting these pages to track your progress, refine your approach to conflict, and celebrate the small victories along the way. The journey to peace and emotional resilience is ongoing—stay committed to your growth, and you will continue to transform your relationships and your life.

Personal Growth Journal:
Date: ____________________

Ongoing Reflections:
Date: ____________________

Emotional Milestones:
Date: ____________________

This journal is your safe space for continuous self-reflection and emotional growth. As you move forward, keep revisiting these pages to track your progress, refine your approach to conflict, and celebrate the small victories along the way. The journey to peace and emotional resilience is ongoing—stay committed to your growth, and you will continue to transform your relationships and your life.

Personal Growth Journal:
Date: ______________

____
____
____
____
____

Ongoing Reflections:
Date: ______________

____
____
____
____
____

Emotional Milestones:
Date: ______________

____
____
____
____
____

This journal is your safe space for continuous self-reflection and emotional growth. As you move forward, keep revisiting these pages to track your progress, refine your approach to conflict, and celebrate the small victories along the way. The journey to peace and emotional resilience is ongoing—stay committed to your growth, and you will continue to transform your relationships and your life.

Personal Growth Journal:

Date: ________________

Ongoing Reflections:
Date: ________________

Emotional Milestones:
Date: ________________

This journal is your safe space for continuous self-reflection and emotional growth. As you move forward, keep revisiting these pages to track your progress, refine your approach to conflict, and celebrate the small victories along the way. The journey to peace and emotional resilience is ongoing—stay committed to your growth, and you will continue to transform your relationships and your life

Conclusion:

From Conflict to Connection—The Power of Transformation.

High-conflict behaviour doesn't just affect moments of disagreement—it seeps into the fabric of relationships, eroding trust, communication, and emotional well-being. It's not merely about the arguments we have but the unspoken fears, insecurities, and unresolved wounds that lie beneath. For too long, we may have seen conflict as an inevitable part of life, something to endure rather than address. But here's the truth: conflict is not an unchangeable force. It is a call to action, a signal that something deeper is stirring, asking to be understood, healed, and transformed.

Breaking the Cycle Starts Here.

For those struggling with high-conflict tendencies, the power to change lies within. It starts with recognizing your emotional triggers and understanding how your past may be influencing your present reactions. High-conflict personalities are often born out of deep fears—fear of abandonment, rejection, or not being enough. But these fears don't have to define you. You can learn new skills, build emotional intelligence, and practice self-regulation, transforming the way you engage with others. You can choose peace over chaos, connection over isolation.

For those living or working with high-conflict individuals, the journey is about creating space—space for empathy, understanding, and boundaries. It's about realizing that you cannot change someone else, but you can influence how you engage with them. By setting clear boundaries, refusing to take part in destructive patterns, and encouraging professional help, you open the door to healthier dynamics, where both your needs and theirs can be acknowledged.

Action is the Key to Transformation.

The stories and examples in these chapters are not just windows into others' lives; they are reflections of the challenges we all face in some form. They illustrate that while high-conflict behaviour can feel overwhelming, it doesn't have to be a permanent state. Whether you are the one struggling with conflict or the one affected by it, there is a way forward—a way that leads to growth, understanding, and true connection.

So, What Will You Do Next?

Will you allow conflict to continue ruling your relationships, or will you take the steps to break free from its hold? Will you stay trapped in cycles of defensiveness and anger, or will you learn to pause, reflect, and respond with intention? Will you continue rescuing those you love from their own emotions, or will you empower them to take responsibility for their own growth?

Transformation begins with a single step. Whether it's seeking therapy, practicing mindfulness, setting new boundaries, or learning to communicate with empathy, every small action moves you closer to a life that is not ruled by conflict but enriched by connection. You deserve relationships built on respect, trust, and mutual understanding. You deserve peace.

The storm doesn't have to last forever. Choose to calm it. Choose growth, healing, and connection. Choose to transform your life.

Continue post-assessment on next page.

Post-Assessment.

"Taming the Storm:
Understanding and Overcoming High-Conflict Personalities for a Peaceful Life"

The post-assessment is designed to help you track your progress and recognize the shifts in your understanding and approach to high conflict behaviour. Personal growth is a journey that takes practice, patience, and continuous learning. Use this assessment to measure how you're understanding and ability to manage conflict have evolved after reading the book. Reflect on your learning as you answer the following questions.

Reflection Exercise:

Review your scores. Have you noticed any areas of significant improvement? Are there any areas where you feel you need more growth? Write down which chapters or exercises were most impactful for you and which ones you may need to revisit. This reflection can help you identify the next steps in your journey toward managing conflict more effectively.

Goal-Setting Activity:

Based on your assessment, set two specific goals for yourself moving forward. For example, you might commit to practicing mindfulness for five minutes daily or working on expressing your needs more assertively during conflicts. Write down your goals and revisit them regularly to track your progress.

Post-Assessment Scoring Guide.

Scores of 35-50: You've gained significant understanding and skill in managing conflict, both in yourself and with others. You likely feel more confident in setting boundaries and using the tools provided in the book to turn conflict into opportunities for growth and connection.

Scores of 20-34: You've made noticeable progress in your approach to conflict. You may still have areas where you feel challenged, but you are better equipped to handle high conflict situations and continue to build your emotional resilience and communication skills.

Scores of 10-19: While you may still feel that conflict is a significant challenge in your life, you have laid the foundation for further growth. Consider revisiting sections of the book that address emotional regulation, setting boundaries, and communication strategies for continued improvement.

Post-Assessment Questions

On a scale of 1 to 5, how often do you find yourself in arguments or conflicts with others?

(Rarely, Frequently)

After reading this book, how well do you feel you understand the emotional triggers behind your conflicts?

(Not at all, Completely)

How comfortable are you now with expressing your emotions during disagreements?

(Very uncomfortable, Very comfortable)

Have you developed the ability to step back and reflect before responding in a conflict situation?

(Not at all Completely)

Do you feel more equipped to set boundaries in your personal and professional relationships?

(Not at all, Completely)

On a scale of 1 to 5, how often do you still feel personally attacked when others disagree with you?

(Never, Always)

Have you improved your ability to stay calm and manage emotions when faced with high-conflict individuals

(Not at all, Completely)

Do you feel more confident that conflict can be transformed into an opportunity for personal and relational growth?

(Not confident at all, Very confident)

After reading this book, how well do you understand the role of personality disorders in high-conflict behaviour?

(Not at all, Completely)

Do you now feel more capable of handling high-conflict situations without compromising your emotional well-being?

(Not at al ,Completely)

Biography: Hasan Clay.

Hasan Clay is a Certified Professional Life Coach with a 15-year track record of delivering compassionate, results-driven strategies for overall mental health. His approach focuses on guiding individuals through a transformative, customized journey. Specializing in group and individual counseling, Hasan's methods emphasize finding immediate solutions while employing a long-term, results-oriented perspective. He offers support for challenges like anxiety, depression, anger management, PTSD, crisis prevention, and more.

Hasan holds a bachelor's degree in psychology, a master's in business administration, and a Doctorate in Business Administration (DBA). His journey is marked by overcoming personal adversity, which fuels his passion for helping others. Raised primarily by a single mother, Hasan dropped out of high school and became entangled in the school-to-prison pipeline at the age of 20. Through patience, prayer, and perseverance, he re-entered society, excelling in education and becoming a productive community member, only to face the challenge of losing his eyesight later in life. Through these trials and triumphs, he continued advocating for his clients, using his story as a testament to resilience and growth.

Hasan's approach is holistic, incorporating a focus on men's mental health while also advocating for inclusivity and equity for women and marginalized communities. In couples and family counseling, he offers guidance for men to become grounded in their masculinity while providing women with insight into the male perspective, helping them position themselves from a place of strength.

Core Beliefs and Approach

Hasan's spiritual beliefs are a driving force in his work ethic. However, the level of spiritual interaction in his sessions is client driven, ensuring a safe space for all faith-based communities. His personal investment in each client, balanced with professionalism, creates a healing environment that is second to none. He combines real-world experience and academic expertise to guide clients from diverse backgrounds toward success.

Professional Experience:

Hasan has worked with various organizations, including the Georgia Lawyers Foundation, Morehouse School of Medicine, Emory University, and the Georgia State Prisons. He has supported clients across 18 countries and collaborated with a variety of interfaith and spiritual organizations.

Availability:

Hasan is available for speaking engagements, workshops, and one-on-one coaching. He believes in using practical strategies and a compassionate approach to help individuals and groups break free from conflict patterns and achieve emotional well-being.

Reflection Prompt:

Hasan's journey is a story of resilience, transformation, and growth. Reflect on how his experiences might resonate with your own challenges. Consider how his approach could guide you in creating a more balanced and peaceful life for yourself.

Glossary.

Active Listening.

A communication technique that involves giving full attention to the speaker without interrupting or planning your response. The listener reflects what they hear to ensure understanding and shows empathy. Example: During a disagreement, instead of jumping in with your point, try saying, "What I hear you saying is..." and repeat what the other person expressed. This builds trust and reduces misunderstandings.

Anxiety.

a state of anxiety, uneasiness, or concern, often caused by a situation where the outcome is unclear. Anxiety can be a driver of high conflict behaviour when individuals feel overwhelmed and unable to manage their emotions effectively.

Reflection Prompt: Think about the last time you felt anxious. How did it impact your behaviour or interactions with others?

Attachment Style

A pattern of forming relationships based on childhood interactions with caregivers. Common styles include secure, anxious, avoidant, and disorganized. People with insecure attachment styles may struggle more with high-conflict behaviour due to fears of abandonment or rejection.

Simplified Explanation:

If you find yourself either clinging to others or pushing them away during conflicts, your attachment style might be influencing your reactions.

Boundaries:

Set clear boundary limits or rules set in relationships to protect your mental health. Boundaries help you figure out what is acceptable behaviour from others and what isn't. Setting boundaries is crucial in managing high-conflict situations and maintaining emotional health. Example: "I'm not comfortable discussing this when you raise your voice. Let's talk when we're both calm."

Cognitive-Behavioural Therapy (CBT)

A type of therapy that focuses on changing negative thought patterns and behaviours. CBT helps individuals identify their emotional triggers and develop healthier responses.

Application:

If you often feel attacked during disagreements, CBT techniques can help you reframe those thoughts, allowing you to respond more calmly and effectively.

Conflict Cycle

A repetitive pattern where conflict escalates due to unaddressed emotional triggers and defensive behaviours. Understanding the cycle can help individuals break free from unproductive habits and create more peaceful interactions.

Reflection Exercise:

Identify the last three conflicts you had. Were there any patterns in your reactions or the topics that triggered you? Noticing these patterns is the first step toward change.

Dialectical behaviour Therapy (DBT):

A therapeutic approach designed to help people manage intense emotions, often used for individuals with borderline personality disorder (BPD). DBT combines mindfulness practices with techniques for emotional regulation and interpersonal effectiveness.

Simplified Definition:

DBT teaches people how to stay present and manage overwhelming emotions so they can respond thoughtfully instead of reacting impulsively.

Empathy:

The ability to feel others' emotions and share the feelings of another person. Empathy plays a vital role in managing conflicts, as it allows individuals to see beyond their perspective and connect with others on a deeper level.

Practice Exercise:

The next time someone expresses frustration, try to imagine yourself in their situation and ask, "How might I feel if I were in their shoes?"

Emotional Regulation:

The ability to manage and respond to your emotional experiences in a healthy way. Emotional regulation techniques, such as deep breathing or

mindfulness, are essential for reducing the intensity of conflict and making thoughtful decisions.
Example: When you feel your temper rising, taking five deep breaths can help calm your nervous system and create a moment to reflect before responding.

High-Conflict Personality:

A term used to describe individuals who frequently engage in intense or confrontational behaviour. This may be driven by deep-seated fears, insecurities, or personality disorders.

Reflection Prompt:

If you or someone you know often turns minor issues into major conflicts, consider what underlying emotions might be fuelling these reactions.

Insecurity:

A feeling of uncertainty or lack of confidence, often tied to fears of rejection or failure. Insecurity can lead to defensive behaviours and conflicts as individuals try to protect themselves from perceived threats.

Example: If you find yourself lashing out when criticized, it could be a sign that insecurity is at play, making you feel vulnerable.

Mindfulness

A practice of being fully present and fully engaged in the moment, without judgment. Mindfulness can help individuals recognize emotional triggers and choose thoughtful responses rather than reacting impulsively.

Application:
Practicing mindfulness for five minutes a day can increase your awareness of how your emotions influence your behaviour, helping you manage conflicts more effectively.

Narcissistic Personality Disorder (NPD)

A personality disorder characterized by an excessive need for admiration, a lack of empathy, and a pattern of grandiosity. Individuals with NPD may struggle with criticism and react defensively, often escalating conflicts.

Simplified Explanation:

If someone frequently shifts the blame or refuses to take responsibility in conflicts, they might have traits associated with narcissistic personality disorder. (For more details, see the chapter on personality disorders.

Non-Defensive Communication:

A technique that focuses on expressing feelings without blaming others. This approach helps de-escalate conflict and promotes open, respectful dialogue.

Example: Instead of saying, "You never listen to what I have to say," try, "I don't feel heard when I'm interrupted." This shifts the focus to your experience without attacking the other person.

Personality Disorders:

Long-term patterns of thinking, feeling, and behaving that are rigid and often lead to difficulties in relationships. Personality disorders, such as borderline personality disorder (BPD) or narcissistic personality disorder (NPD), can intensify conflicts due to their impact on emotions and behaviour.

Reflection Prompt:

If you or a loved one struggles with intense emotional swings or recurring conflicts, consider seeking professional help to understand if a personality disorder may be influencing behaviour.

Reframing:

A cognitive technique that involves changing the way you view a situation to alter its emotional impact. Reframing helps reduce the intensity of conflicts by shifting focus from negative assumptions to more constructive perspectives.

Practice Exercise:

The next time you feel slighted, pause and ask yourself, “What else could this mean?” This helps you see alternative interpretations that are less emotionally charged.

Self-Awareness:

The ability to recognize and understand your own emotions, thinking, and behaviours. Developing self-awareness is the first step toward managing conflict effectively, as it allows individuals to identify their triggers and patterns.

Reflection Prompt:

At the end of each day, write down one moment where you felt emotional. What triggered it, and how did you react? This can help you identify patterns over time.

Therapeutic Support:

Professional guidance, such as counseling or therapy, is aimed at helping individuals understand and manage their emotions, behaviours, and conflicts. Different types of therapy, including CBT and DBT, offer specific tools for addressing high-conflict behaviour.

Simplified Definition:

Therapy provides a space to explore your emotions, understand your patterns, and develop strategies for healthier interactions.

Triggers:

Emotional stimuli that provoke a strong reaction, often tied to past experiences or unresolved emotions. Understanding and managing triggers are crucial steps in reducing conflict and creating more positive interactions.

Example: If a particular tone of voice consistently upsets you, it may be a trigger tied to past experiences. Identifying it allows you to prepare and respond differently when it arises again.

Vulnerability:

The willingness to show emotions and share your true thoughts, even when it feels uncomfortable. Vulnerability is often perceived as a weakness, but it is a strength that allows for deeper connection and understanding in relationships.

Reflection Exercise:

Think of a time when you shared your feelings openly. How did it impact your relationship with the other person? Did it lead to greater connection or understanding?

Made in the USA
Columbia, SC
07 April 2025

56158805R00065